Learning VIM Gently

Sujata Biswas

Content

Introduction to VI and VIM

For decades, VI has been a ubiquitous text editor in the Linux and UNIX communities, and it remains an indispensable tool for system administrators who need to edit configuration files. Despite the availability of numerous GUI text editors like gedit, VI and its modern counterpart, VIM, have endured as the go-to tools for many in the industry.

In this book, we will explore the power of VI and VIM, and demonstrate how these editors can be used for more than just simple text editing. They are highly efficient tools for documentation and offer a range of advanced features that can help streamline your workflow.

One of the most significant advantages of VI and VIM is that they can be used over a network via ssh or telnet commands, making them an excellent choice for remote access scenarios. Additionally, these editors are lightweight and consume minimal system resources, which is especially important in resource-constrained environments.

VIM, in particular, is a worthy successor to VI, offering expanded functionalities and the ability to run on almost all major operating systems, including Linux, OS/2, and more. In a sense, VIM is the modern version of VI, designed to meet the needs of today's technology landscape.

Whether you are a seasoned Linux administrator or a new user looking to explore VI and VIM, this book will provide you with the knowledge and practical skills you need to master these powerful tools. Join us on this journey, and discover the many benefits of VI and VIM.

Installation of VIM on Ubuntu

If you do not already have VIM, then you must install it on your Ubuntu system. The reason you may not have **vim** installed on Ubuntu is that during the installation you selected Minimal Install. You probably have **vi** but not **vim**.

Type **vim** in your terminal window:

$ vim

If you get an output like:

The program 'vim' can be found in the following packages:
 * vim
 * vim-gnome
 * vim-tiny
 * vim-athena
 * vim-athena-py2
 * vim-gnome-py2
 * vim-gtk
 * vim-gtk-py2
 * vim-gtk3
 * vim-gtk3-py2
 * vim-nox
 * vim-nox-py2
Try: sudo apt install <selected package>

You should install **vim** in the following manner. In Ubuntu, there is no root user, so, you must use the **sudo** command to install **vim** or any other software for that matter:

$ sudo apt-get install vim

You will be asked for your password and then permission to install the package. Go ahead and type **y**:

The following NEW packages will be installed:
  vim vim-runtime
0 upgraded, 2 newly installed, 0 to remove and 243 not upgraded.
Need to get 6,199 kB of archives.
After this operation, 30.0 MB of additional disk space will be used.
Do you want to continue? [Y/n]

To verify that **vim** is installed, enter **which** command followed by **vim**, this gives you the absolute path to the location of **vim** on your system:

$ which vim
/usr/bin/vim

Along with **vim**, there are other dependencies and binaries that are also installed. Check the contents of **/usr/bin** with **ls /usr/bin vi*** command

$ ls /usr/bin vi*

vi   viewer vim   vimdiff vimtutor   vino-preferences
view viewres vim.basic vim.tiny

There is a tutorial that you can use to learn about **vim** called **vimtutor.**

To run **vimtutor**, just type it on the command line:

$ vimtutor

After you had verified the **vim** installation, type **vim** on the terminal and you should see the following snapshot:

```
                    VIM - Vi IMproved

                    version 7.4.1689
                 by Bram Moolenaar et al.
      Modified by pkg-vim-maintainers@lists.alioth.debian.org
          Vim is open source and freely distributable

              Become a registered Vim user!
      type   :help register<Enter>      for information

      type   :q<Enter>                  to exit
      type   :help<Enter>   or   <F1>   for on-line help
      type   :help version7<Enter>      for version info
```

The screenshot is showing the **vim** version 7.4.1689

As you can see, VIM is derived from Vi IMproved.

Note: In Centos, the command that you will use to install **vim** is **yum** instead of **apt-get**. You need root access to install **vim**.

yum install vim

Working with VIM

Start **vim** with a file name. Let's start with a new file called **testfile**. If the file did not exist **vim** creates the file.

$ vim testfile

```
"testfile" [New File]                                    0,0-1           All
```

The screenshot shows the opening of a new file in **vim**

You can see the name of the file at the bottom. The **vim** opens in the command mode. In this mode, you cannot type any content in the file. You must enter **i** to enter the insert mode. When you type **i**, the word INSERT appears instead of the file name:

```
-- INSERT --                                              0,1              All
```

The screenshot is showing the INSERT mode, note the INSERT at the bottom of the screen

At this mode, you can type any content that you want. After you had entered your desired content, you need to go back to the command mode. You do that by pressing the **esc** key. As soon as you press the **esc** key, the word INSERT vanishes from the bottom. Now, you have re-entered the command mode.

The screenshot is showing the Command mode after escaping from the insert mode by keying **esc** key

The next step is to enter the colon, **:**, to enter the commands. You can see that a colon has appeared along with the green cursor. Type **w** for write and **q** for quitting the file.

The screenshot is showing the activation of the last-line command mode by keying in : (colon).

What you are doing (by keying **wq**) is writing the content to the **testfile** and quitting **vim**.

```
This is a test file to learn about VIM.
~
~
~
~
~
~
~
~
~
~
~
~
~
~
~
~
~
~
:wq!
```

The screenshot is showing a step before exiting the file by inputting **wq!** last-line command.

Now, you are back in the command line; you see a file called **testfile** created. Check the content of the **testfile** with the **cat** command.

$ ls testfile

testfile

$ cat testfile

This is a test file to learn about vim

In this book, **vim**'s three modes of operation will be studied. Which are:

- Command or normal
- Insert
- Last-line mode

Command mode: You enter this mode as soon as you enter **vim** on the command line. It will not take any input from you. It takes only special commands that you learn letter.

Note: The command mode is also called the normal mode. So, don't get confused. This is the default mode when you open a file.

Insert and Last-line modes: To enter this mode, you must enter **i**, the INSERT word appears at the bottom of your screen to signify that you are in INSERT mode. In this mode, you either add or edit or delete content depending on whether you have opened a new or an old file. After you had finished your work, **you need to re-enter the command mode by pressing the esc key**. You are in command mode. To quit the file, press the **:** (colon) key and **w** (for writing) and **q** (for quitting).

Colon is a Last-line command mode. Moreover, the commands, **w** or **q** are also called last-line commands.

Note: Besides the **i** key, you can also enter the INSERT mode by pressing the **o** key. However, the **o** key will add a line right below. There is also another INSERT command called **a** (append).

Let's test the **o** command

$ vim testfile2

```
This is a test to check the command-mode command o
This is a test to check the command-mode command a
```

The screenshot shows the state of the file before application of the **o** command

Instead of **i** command to go the insert mode, key in **o**, which not only places your file in Insert mode but creates an empty line below the line where the cursor is.

```
This is a test to check the command-mode command o

This is a test to check the command-mode command a
```

The screenshot shows the state of the file after the **o** command and the new line created by the command.

If you want to add something at the end of the line, then take the cursor to the end of the line and use the **a** command. It takes you to the INSERT mode and lets you add content. The **a** is the append command.

Navigation commands

Navigation and Manipulation of text in the file is the topic of discussion in this section.

Command w

Open the file created in the last section:

$ vim testfile

The file opens in the command mode, as usual; you cannot see any content. Now, to navigate between words, type **w** (it will not show up on your screen).

The cursor will be on the letter "T" of "This" when you type **w** again; the cursor goes to "i" of "is" , type **w** again, the cursor goes to "a" and so forth.

The underscore represents the cursor in the following example and shows the how pressing **w** moves from one word to another:

This is a test file to learn about vim

The **w** command moves from left to right. To navigate between words, you may also use the **e** command, instead of traversing words by the first letter, **e** travels by the last letter. It can be represented as

This is a test file to learn about vim

Note 1: Do not confuse this **w** command with the command you learned earlier to write to the file. The other **w** which you put after the colon is the last-line command.

Note 2: You may use the right, left, top and bottom keyboard arrow keys in the text area when you are in the command mode. There are keys which assigned to these operations, look at the following table.

Command-line command	Arrow-key equivalent
h	Left
j	Up
k	Down
l	Right

Command b

The command **b** is the exact opposite of **w**; it retracts back, moves back between words in the opposite direction to **w**. When you open the file for the first time, it does not work, because (obviously) it cannot move back.

The **b** command moves from right to left.

You need to type **Shift + $** to go to the end of the line in the command mode. These commands will not work in the insert mode.

```
This is a test file to learn about vim
~
```

Showing the effect of **Shift + $**, the cursor goes to the end of the line.

Now, to go to the beginning of the line, press 0 (the numerical)

```
This is a test file to learn about vim
```

The screenshot shows that the cursor returns to the beginning of the line with 0 (zero)

You should use **Shift + m** (middle) and **Shift + l** (lower end of the screen) to go to the middle of the screen. Again, this command works when you open the file, and you are in the command mode.

If you wish to go to back to the beginning of the screen the command is **Shift + nh.**

G (capital) moves to the end of the file. While **g** (small) to the beginning of the file. It is a useful set of commands to remember while dealing with long files.

You can use **G** to go to specific line number as well. Type numerical **6 + G** and the cursor goes to line **6**.

```
This is line 1
This is line 2
This is line 3
This is line 4
This is line 5
This is line 6
```

The screenshot is showing the result of the **6+G** command

Note: Adding a number before the command is called multiple-iterations of the command. It is one of the most helpful features of **vim**.

Editing commands

Deleting one character using x

For deleting in the command mode, you use the **x** command. Place the cursor on the character you want to delete and type **x**, keep on typing **x** to delete characters to the right one by one. Space is also considered a character. If you wish to delete 10 characters to the right, you should use **10 + x**.

Note: **+** doesn't mean that you put input + from the keyboard. It is that the two commands need to be run together.

Deleting a whole word using dw command

Place the cursor on the first character of the word and type **dw** in command mode. See the screenshot, where the cursor is on the character **l** of line.

```
This is line 1
This is line 2
This is line 3
This is line 4
This is line 5
This is line 6
```

The screenshot shows the selection of the word that is to be deleted.

After you type **dw**; the word line vanishes from the screen:

```
This is line 1
This is line 2
This is 3
This is line 4
This is line 5
This is line 6
```

The screenshot shows that word line has been deleted.

You can also use it to delete several words, let's suppose you want to delete the next three words from the point you place the cursor on. In this example, the cursor is on This of line 4; the intent is to delete "This" and then the next 2 words which are "is" and "line."

$ vim testfile1

```
This is line 1
This is line 2
This is line 3
This is line 4
This is line 5
This is line 6
```

The command will be **3dw**, as you can see the three words "This", "is" and "line" are deleted.

```
This is line 1
This is line 2
This is line 3
4
This is line 5
This is line 6
```

The screenshot shows the deletion of 3 words using **3dw**

Note: The example file is being reused, the file is not being saved after the delete operations. To do the same:

- To go to the insert mode, type **i**
- Type **:**
- Just after, **:**, type, **q!** to exit out of the file without saving. The exclamation mark is force quit without saving.

This is a handy command to delete a whole line. Place the cursor at the beginning of the line and type **dd** to delete the whole line. Multiple lines can also be deleted by placing a number before **dd**. If you want to delete 4 lines, then the command will **4+dd**. Remember, that an empty line is also a "line" for **vim**.

Notice the placement of the cursor in the following snapshot, which is on the word like.

```
This is line 1. I have got Monday Blues.
This is line 2. I don't want to go to office
This is line 3. I like my boss.
This is line 4. Have a nice day.
This is line 5. Today is Friday. What a relief.
This is line 6. Today is Saturday
```

The screenshot shows the selection of a portion of the line is deleted.

If you want partially to delete the line from the start of the line until the placement of the cursor, then type **d + Zero**, notice the in the following screenshot, you can see that words before the word **like** have been deleted.

```
This is line 1. I have got Monday Blues.
This is line 2. I don't want to go to office
like my boss.
This is line 4. Have a nice day.
This is line 5. Today is Friday. What a relief.
This is line 6. Today is Saturday
```

In real life if you have made a mistake, you can undo the changes, for that:

- Press **esc** to go command mode – just to make sure, even if you are in the command mode.
- Type :
- Type **u** after the: and enter.

In the previous example, you learned to delete the line from the beginning of the line to the point where the cursor was on. The next command will be from the point the cursor was on to the end of the line. The command is **d+Shift+$** in the command mode.

The intent is to delete rest of the line, till the end. Notice the placement of the cursor in the following screenshot:

```
This is line 1. I have got Monday Blues.
This is line 2. I don't want to go to office
This is line 3. I like my boss.
This is line 4. Have a nice day.
This is line 5. Today is Friday. What a relief.
This is line 6. Today is Saturday
```

Everything from "**s**" of "**is**" should be deleted by **d+Shift+$**

```
This is line 1. I have got Monday Blues.
This is line 2. I don't want to go to office
This is line 3. I like my boss.
This is line 4. Have a nice day.
This is line 5. Today i
This is line 6. Today is Saturday
```

Note: Do not practice on live production servers and avoid playing around with configuration files in **/etc** directory. If you have no other options available, then do make a copy (or two) of the file first and then play around – but this is also dangerous.

Redo command

In the last section, you were introduced to the undo command **u**. There is also the redo command, which represented by the period (dot .) symbol.

- Open a file
- Add some text in the INSERT mode. Make sure that the cursor is at the beginning of the text.
- Key **esc** to go to the Command mode
- Press the period (dot) key to repeat the text you added.

Note: The . (dot) is not going to repeat the stuff you typed earlier. It will repeat the last command.

Additional Editing commands

In this section, you will learn about the **r** and **cc** commands to be run on command mode of **vim**.

The **r** command replaces a character at a time:

Open the file. Place the cursor on the character you want to change/replace. I often use this in a shell script for minor typographical errors that may lead to the script failing to run. Check the very simple script below. The script, **jackpot.sh**, takes a number from the standard input (what you type) and if the number is more than 10, echoes a message " You have won the jackpot".

#!/bin/bash

echo " Enter a number: "
read number

if (($numver > 10))
then
        echo " You won the jackpot"
fi

When you try to run the script after giving it the executable permission, you get a syntax error after you input a number more than 10

$ chmod u+x jackpot.sh

$ ./jackpot.sh

 Enter a number:

11 # <- The number you enter

./jackpot.sh: line 6: ((: > 10 : syntax error: operand expected (error token is "> 10 ")

If you check the script again, you can see that the variable "number" is misspelled in the code.

Open the script jackpot.sh in **vim**, place the cursor in v of "numver" to change it to b.

```
#!/bin/bash

echo " Enter a number: "
read number

if (( $numver > 10 ))
then
        echo " You won the jackpot"
fi
```

The screenshot shows the application of the **r** command correcting the spelling of the number

Now, type **r** followed by the letter you want to replace (in this case **b)** in the script. Moreover, exit out of the script by saving it using: **wq**

Just because the variable is misspelled, the whole script fails!

Similar to **dd** (which deletes the line(s)), there is a command called **cc**, open the file in vim, place the cursor on a line that you want to delete, type **cc**, not only the line is deleted, but you find yourself in the insert mode.

For copying and pasting, two commands are used:

- **yy** command for copying an entire line. The y stands for yanking.
- **p** command for pasting

Consider, the file that you have used before:

This is line 1. I have got Monday Blues.
This is line 2. I do not want to go to the office
This is line 3. I like my boss.
This is line 4. Have a nice day.
This is line 5. Today is Friday. What a relief.
This is line 6. Today is Saturday

To copy a single line:

- Place the cursor at the beginning of the line and type **yy**
- Go to the place where you want to copy that in. You may have to go to the insert mode by tying **i** and then place the cursor in the desired place. Also, remember to press **esc** to activate the **p** (pasting) command.

To copy multiple lines:

- Place the cursor at the beginning of the line, decide how many lines you want to copy and enter the **Nyy** command. N stands for some lines. If you want to copy the next 5 lines, the command will be **5yy**. You will notice the following message at the bottom of the screen:

```
5 lines yanked
```

The screenshot shows the yanking message at the bottom of the screen

- Go to the place where you want to copy that in. You may have to go insert mode by typing **i,** place the cursor at the desired location, revert to the command mode by pressing esc key and type **p** to paste.

Note: Use capital **P** to paste content before the cursor. The **p** command pastes the content after the cursor.

Using the y command in Visual mode

This section is the sub-set of the previous section "Copying and pasting."

This section has the dual purpose of showing you another mode of **vim** called the Visual mode and using the **y** command (single yank) to copy selected text. You do not need to copy the whole line from one location to another. You may want to copy the partial content of a line.

- Open a file using **vim**
- Go to a line and put the cursor on a word you want to select
- Key in **v**, notice that the bottom of the screen says VISUAL
- Now using the Shift or the right arrow key select the content. Notice that it gets highlighted. When you have finished, key in **y** to copy
- Place the cursor where you want to copy and key in the paste command, **p**.

The screenshot shows the bottom of the screen displaying VISUAL and the highlighting of the text after **v** command

Substitution command

Reusing the file **testfile1** again:

This is line 1. I have got Monday Blues.
This is line 2. I do not want to go to the office
This is line 3. I like my boss.
This is line 4. Have a nice day.
This is line 5. Today is Friday. What a relief.
This is line 6. Today is Saturday

The substitution uses the last-line command **s**. You open the file with **vim** and press the colon key. Now, you are in the last-line command mode. To start substitution, use the following syntax:

:s/pattern/replacement

So, if you want to replace **the line** with **fine**, the command will be:

:s/line/fine

The file will look like:

This is fine 1. I have got Monday Blues.
This is line 2. I do not want to go to the office
This is line 3. I like my boss.
This is line 4. Have a nice day.
This is line 5. Today is Friday. What a relief.
This is line 6. Today is Saturday

Depending on where your cursor is, the line will be substituted by fine. If you wish to substitute all the instances of line with fine in that **particular line** (where your cursor is), use:

:s/line/fine/g

To substitute all instances of the line (global) with fine use append **s** with **%**

:%s/line/fine

At the bottom of the screen, you will see the following statement. This is because of 6 instances of the word **line.**

```
~
6 substitutions on 6 lines
```

The screenshot shows the message at the bottom of the screen

The: **%s/line/fine/g** can be an inefficient command. It may replace words which you do not intend to replace. You can use the **c** option along with **g** (global) to ask (your) permission to replace.

The command syntax will be

:%s/the/The/gc

Now, you will see something like:

```
~
replace with fine (y/n/a/q/l/^E/^Y)?
```

The shows the effect of **c** command in :%s/the/The/gc

Note: Though these commands are simple enough but you need to practice a lot. You must be able to toggle between the command and insert mode quickly and efficiently.

Command-line mode commands

You already know about some command-line mode commands/symbols, just to refresh, they are:

- Searching commands Question mark "?" and forward slash "/"
- Filtering command represented by "!"
- On Colon:. Like **w** (for writing to a file), **q** (for quitting) , **u** (for undoing)

Forward slash / for searching

After opening the file, just press **/** and put the pattern you are searching for. The cursor will be on the pattern if found, and for more instances of the same pattern type **n** , till the pattern is no longer found, and it will hit bottom and start from the beginning again. You can perform the same action as **n** if you keep on pressing the **/** key. The search commences from the start of the file until it reaches the end.

Question mark? for searching

Exactly same as forward slash, **/**, however, the searching commences from bottom to the top.

Graphical mode of VIM

The graphical mode of **vim** is enabled and can be used on the console or emulators like NX (no machine) with **vim -g** command.

If you have a minimal install of Ubuntu as I do, then you may see something like this:

$ vim -g

E25: GUI cannot be used: Not enabled at compile time

If you get the error in the previous example, then install the **vim – gnome** package

$ sudo apt-get install vim-gnome

And you either start:

$ vim -g

Alternatively,

$ gvim

Using System commands from vim

You do not even have to leave the **vim** session to execute Linux commands.

Imagine you are creating a report, using this file:

$ vi report.txt

Date is

The content of /etc/hosts file is

Number of users logged in is

Running a command from the vim session

Go to the last-line mode by keying: and then ! and then the Linux command, **date**:

```
Date is
Content of /etc/hosts file is
Number of users logged in is

:!date
```

The screenshot shows how the **date** command is called from **vim**

```
[No write since last change]
Wed Jul  5 20:12:24 IST 2017

Press ENTER or type command to continue
[No write since last change]
Wed Jul  5 20:15:45 IST 2017

Press ENTER or type command to continue
```

The screenshot shows the "**date**" command, and you press Enter to go back to the **vim** session

Reading a command from vim session

If you want to read (using the **r** command) the output of the Linux commands into file opened in **vim**, then you must place the cursor where you want the value of the Linux command and use the following syntax:

: r ! date

And

:r ! cat /etc/hosts

And

:r ! who -u

The file looks like:

Date is

Wed Jul 5 20:20:33 IST 2017

Content of /etc/hosts file is

127.0.0.1   localhost

127.0.1.1   linux1978

 # The following lines are desirable for IPv6 capable hosts

::1   ip6-localhost ip6-loopback

fe00::0 ip6-localnet

ff00::0 ip6-mcastprefix

ff02::1 ip6-allnodes

ff02::2 ip6-allrouters

Number of users logged in is

jeff   tty7   2017-07-04 23:39 20:42   964 (:0)

jeff   pts/11   2017-07-05 15:59 .   20192 (192.168.1.4)

You have now created a whole report without even leaving the **vim** session. What a time-saver!!

Using buffers in VIM

You can employ buffers in **vim** using a command like **saveas**. Any "new" changes in the file is written to a new file.

This is a file called **file1.txt** which has the following content:

$ cat file1.txt

This is file number 1

- Open the file in **vim**
- Add new content
- Type **: saveas newfile1.txt**
- And then: **wq!**

The old file **file1.txt** will not have the new content. The new file that is created by vim will have the new and old content – both.

Navigating and editing text using VIM's marks feature

VIM's marks feature is a powerful tool that allows you to mark specific locations in a file and easily navigate to them later. In this chapter, we will explore how to use VIM's marks feature to efficiently navigate and edit text in your files.

Setting a Mark

To set a mark in VIM, you can use the m command followed by a letter to identify the mark. For example, to set a mark at the current cursor position and label it as "a", you would use the command:

ma

This will set the mark at the current cursor position and label it as "a". You can use any letter from a to z as a mark.

Navigating with Marks

Once you have set a mark in VIM, you can easily navigate to it using the backtick (`) command followed by the mark letter. For example, to quickly jump to mark "a", you would use the command:

`a

This will move the cursor to the line and column where the mark was set.

In addition to using backticks to jump to a specific mark, you can also use the single-quote (') command to jump to the beginning of the line where the mark was set. For example, to jump to the beginning of the line where mark "a" was set, you would use the command:

'a

Deleting Marks

To delete a mark, you can use the command:

:delmarks [marks]

For example, to delete marks "a" and "b", you would use the command:

:delmarks ab

Editing with Marks

VIM's marks feature can also be used to efficiently edit text in your files. For example, you can use marks to quickly select and delete entire sections of text.

To select text between two marks, you can use the command:

`[mark1]v`[mark2]y

For example, to select the text between marks "a" and "b" and copy it to the clipboard, you would use the command:

csharp

Copy code

`av`by

This will select the text between marks "a" and "b" and copy it to the clipboard.

You can also use marks to quickly move and copy text within a file. For example, to move a block of text to a new location in the file, you can use the command:

`[mark1]v`[mark2]d

This will delete the selected text and move the cursor to the location of the first mark. To paste the deleted text at the current cursor position, you can use the command:

p

This will paste the deleted text at the current cursor position.

Undo and redo history in VIM

VIM's undo and redo functionality is an incredibly useful feature that allows you to quickly and easily revert changes that you have made to a file. In this chapter, we will explore how to use VIM's undo and redo history to effectively manage changes to your files.

Undo History

The undo command in VIM allows you to undo the most recent change that you made to a file. This is done using the u command. For example, if you accidentally deleted a line of text, you can use the command:

u

This will undo the deletion and restore the line of text to its original location.

VIM's undo history is not limited to a single change. In fact, VIM keeps a history of all of the changes that you have made to a file, allowing you to easily undo multiple changes at once. You can view the undo history by using the command:

:undolist

This will display a list of all of the changes that you have made to the file, along with the time and date that each change was made. You can then use the u command to undo any of these changes.

In addition to using the u command to undo changes, you can also use the CTRL-r command to redo changes that you have undone. For example, if you accidentally undo a change that you wanted to keep, you can use the command:

objectivec

CTRL-r

This will redo the most recently undone change.

Redo History

VIM's redo history is similar to its undo history, but it allows you to redo changes that you have previously undone. This is done using the CTRL-r command. For example, if you undo a change and then realize that you actually want to keep it, you can use the command:

objectivec

CTRL-r

This will redo the most recently undone change.

VIM's redo history is also not limited to a single change. In fact, VIM keeps a history of all of the changes that you have undone, allowing you to easily redo multiple changes at once. You can view the redo history by using the command:

:redolist

This will display a list of all of the changes that you have undone, along with the time and date that each change was undone. You can then use the CTRL-r command to redo any of these changes.

Advanced Undo and Redo Techniques

In addition to the basic undo and redo functionality that VIM provides, there are also several advanced techniques that you can use to manage changes to your files more effectively.

One technique is to use the g- command to undo changes to a specific line in a file. For example, if you accidentally make changes to a line of text and want to undo those changes, you can use the command:

g-

This will undo the most recent change to the line that the cursor is on.

Another technique is to use the :earlier and :later commands to move backward and forward in time through the undo and redo history. For example, if you want to undo all of the changes that you made in the last hour, you can use the command:

:earlier 1h

This will move the file back in time by one hour, undoing all of the changes that you made during that time period.

Advanced search and replace techniques using regular expressions in VIM

Using macros to automate tasks in VIM

Working with multiple windows and tabs in VIM

Integrating VIM with other tools and applications, such as Git or Tmux

Scripting in VIM using Vimscript or Python

Working with syntax highlighting and code folding in VIM

Tips and tricks for efficient editing and navigation in VIM.